The Story of a Special Day
Volume 231

August
18

The 230th day of the year (231st in leap years).
There are 135 days remaining until the end of the year.

by Michael Dobson

Timespinner
Press

This book is also available in e-book form for Kindle, e-pub devices, and other formats from your favorite online booksellers.

For more information about the series, about us, or about your special day, please email us at editor@timespinnerpress.com.

Look for other volumes in *The Story of a Special Day*, coming often. See www.timespinnerpress.com for details and for the most recent information.

Table of Contents

**For the definition of "O.S.," "CE," and "BCE" used with
some dates , see the section "On Names and Dates."**

Cover: Detail from the official program for the 1913 Women's
Suffrage Procession in Washington, DC, by Benjamin Moran Dale.
The 19th Amendment to the US Constitution, giving women the right
to vote, was ratified August 18, 1920 — the **Event of the Day**.

Quote of the Day

"In the new Code of Laws which I suppose it will be necessary for you to make I desire you would Remember the Ladies, and be more generous and favourable to them than your ancestors. ...

If particular care and attention is not paid to the Ladies we are determined to foment a Rebellion, and will not hold ourselves bound by any Laws in which we have no voice, or Representation."

Abigail Adams, wife of US President John Adams, in 1776. US women received the right to vote with the passage of the 19th Amendment on August 18, 1920

Today in History

August 18

Elizabeth Cady Stanton (seated) and Susan B. Anthony

Event of the Day
August 18, 1920 — US Women Get the Right to Vote

The Nineteenth Amendment to the US Constitution was ratified on August 18, 1920.

Amendment XIX. The right of citizens of the United States to vote shall not be denied or abridged by the United States or by any State on account of sex. Congress shall have the power to enforce this article by appropriate legislation.

Women and the Vote

In a world where most governments were dominated by a very few, the right to vote (suffrage) was tightly held, and then mostly by men. With a few exceptions, women were routinely denied suffrage.

With the spread of modern democracy, the right to vote became more important and more widespread, though women were still typically excluded. Sweden permitted women to vote between 1718 and 1772. Some smaller nations also allowed women voting.

The first legal woman voter in colonial America was Massachusetts resident Lydia Taft. She is recorded as having voted at least three times.

The Women's Suffrage Movement in America

The original 1789 US Constitution did not specify who was entitled to vote, and delegated voter qualifications to the states. Of the original US states, only New Jersey allowed women to vote, but that changed in 1807. The Kingdom of Hawai'i, prior to annexation, gave women the right to vote in 1840, but rescinded it in 1852.

The battle for women's suffrage took place in a number of nations. In the United States, the movement is considered to have begun in 1840 at the World Anti-Slavery Convention, when delegates Elizabeth Cady Stanton and Lucretia Mott were denied seating because of their sex.

In 1848, Stanton helped organize the Seneca Falls Convention, dedicated to women's issues. The convention received national attention, and other women's conventions followed.

Two national women's suffrage associations led the fight. Stanton, along with Susan B. Anthony, formed the National Woman Suffrage Association (NWSA), and Julia Ward Howe, Lucy Stone, and others formed the American Woman Suffrage Association (AWSA).

The split between the two was about strategy. AWSA favored going state-by-state to achieve women's suffrage.

NWSA, on the other hand, wanted a constitutional strategy. Originally, their campaign was to have the proposed Fifteenth Amendment, prohibited the denial of suffrage based on race, changed to "race or sex."

After the Fifteenth Amendment was ratified as originally written, the two organizations eventually patched up their differences and merged in 1890. They tried a legal strategy that argued the Fourteenth Amendment implicitly protected a woman's right to vote, but the argument was rejected by the Supreme Court.

Susan B. Anthony became a test case, and was arrested for voting in the 1872 presidential election. She was denied the right to speak during the trial, though after the guilty verdict was rendered, gave a passionate speech in her defense. Fined $100, she replied, "I shall never pay a dollar of your unjust penalty," and she never did.

Women's Suffrage parade in New York City, 1912

The Nineteenth Amendment

The Nineteenth Amendment was introduced in 1878 by Senator Aaron A. Sargent of California, a friend of Susan B. Anthony and himself a women's suffrage advocate. (He was also known as the "Senator for the Southern Pacific Railroad.")

Sargent had previously attempted to slip women's suffrage into unrelated bills, but had been unsuccessful. After numerous hearings and delays, the amendment was brought before the full senate in 1887. The vote was 16 for and 34 against.

Meanwhile, the fight at the state level moved forward. A number of women's suffrage bills had been introduced in various state legislatures after 1840, but few even came to a vote. Beginning in 1910, however, a number of western states, including California and Washington, enfranchised women voters.

"The Awakening," by Hy Mayer, showing the advancement of women's suffrage in the United States (1915)

This resulted in the Senate reconsidering the Nineteenth Amendent in 1914. It was again rejected.

During World War I, the suffrage movement split again on support for the war, as many members were pacifists. One part of the movement supported the war effort while the other organized a series of controversial demonstrations, resulting in numerous arrests, hunger strikes, and mob violence against demonstrators.

More and more, support was building. President Woodrow Wilson endorsed the amendment, leading to another vote in 1918. This one passed the House but fell two votes short in the Senate; the next year another attempt was made but this time failed by only one vote.

President Wilson called a special session of Congress a few months later to vote yet again, and this time it was successful. Within days, Illinois, Wisconsin, and Michigan ratified the amendment.

By the end of 1919, 22 out of the necessary 36 states had ratified the amendment. The following year, enough additional states had ratified the amendment so that it became part of the Constitution. Tennessee was the 36th state to do so, ratifying the amendment.

Although it was not necessary for the remaining states to ratify it, eventually they all did, with Mississippi doing so last in 1984 (after rejecting it in 1920). Hawaii and Alaska have not ratified the

amendment because it was already part of the
Constitution when they gained statehood.

Women's Suffrage headquarters in Cleveland, 1912

Aftermath

A 1922 lawsuit, Leser v. Garnett, argued that the
ratification was faulty, but the Supreme Court
unanimously upheld the new amendment's validity.

Initially, relatively few women exercised their
new right, with 36% of eligible women voting, as
opposed to 68% of men.

This was at least partially due to common
barriers to voting, such as poll taxes and literacy
tests, along with general inexperience and a belief by
part of society that voting was inappropriate
behavior for women. More importantly, laws

designed to keep black men from voting also kept black women from doing so.

By 1964, however, the situation was reversed, and in every presidential election from then on, the number of female voters exceeded the number of male voters. Starting in 1980, the proportion of female voters has also exceeded the proportion of voting males.

Postcard promoting women's suffrage, circa 1913

"The 1783 Great Meteor as seen from Windsor Castle," watercolor by Paul Sandby.

A British Observer Corps aircraft spotter on the roof of a London building during the Battle of Britain.

What Happened on August 18?

From great works of engineering and art to devastating wars and natural disasters, thousands of years of history have left their mark on each and every day of the year. Here are some important events that occurred on August 18. (Items with a photo or illustration are boxed.)

1587 — **Virginia Dare** becomes the first English child born in the Americas.

1612 — The **Pendle witch trials**, one of the most famous in British history, begins. Of the thirteen accused women and men, ten were hanged.

1783 — The **Great Meteor of 1783**, a bolide (meteor that explodes in the atmosphere) twice as bright as a full moon, is sighted, causing much speculation because the phenomenon was not then well understood.

1868 — **Helium is discovered** by French astronomer Pierre Janssen.

1940 — During the Battle of Britain, the engagement known as the **Hardest Day** takes place. Both British and German forces lose more aircraft than on any other single day during the campaign. *(Also next page.)*

1945 — Sukarno takes office as **first president of Indonesia**; he remains in office until 1967.

Official portrait of President Sukarno of Indonesia

1958 — Vladimir Nabokov's controversial novel *Lolita* **is published** in the United States.

1977— Anti-apartheid activist **Steve Biko is arrested** in South Africa; he later dies from injuries resulting from his arrest.

British Hawker Hurricanes during the Battle of Britain

German Heinkel He 111s during the Battle of Britain

Quote of the Day

"The more a man judges, the less he loves."

Honoré de Balzac, .novelist
died August 18, 1850

Births
and
Deaths

August 18

Baseball Hall of Fame pitcher Burleigh Grimes, the last pitcher officially allowed to throw the spitball after it was banned in 1920. He was born on August 18, 1893

Notable August 18 People

With the current world population at about seven billion people, on average about 19 million people also celebrate their birthdays on August 18 — and that isn't counting millions and millions who came before! No matter when you were born, you share your birthday with many special people whose accomplishments (and occasionally embarrassments) have been noted as part of history.

In this section, you'll meet fascinating people who share your birthday. They're organized by what they're famous for, and then in reverse chronological order from most recent to earliest. Those who are shown in photographs or artwork have a box around them. We don't have photos of everyone, so please forgive us if your favorite person is missing.

Some of these people you've heard of, others will be new to you, but they all make up an important part of the reason that August 18 is a truly special day!

Marshall Field

Who Was Born on August 18?

Activism

Amelia Boynton Robinson, civil rights leader and key figure in the 1965 Selma-to-Montgomery marches, played by Lorraine Toussaint in the2014 film *Selma. (1911)*

Margaret Murie, naturalist and author considered the "grandmother of the conservation movement" by the Sierra Club and the Wilderness Society; received the Audobon Medal, the John Muir Award, and the Presidential Medal of Freedom. *(1902)*

Business

Marshall Field, founded the Chicago-based chain of department stores that carry his name. *(1834)*

Journalism and Literature

Bob Woodruff, co-anchor of ABC World News Tonight; wounded by a bomb in Iraq. *(1961)*

Vincent Bugliosi, best-selling author of true crime and political books; previously a successful district attorney whose most famous case was the prosecution of Charles Manson. *(1934)*

Brian Aldiss, English science fiction writer and editor, member of the Science Fiction Hall of Fame. *(1925)*

Military and Exploration

Lydia Litvyak (Лидия Литвяк), Soviet air force pilot who was the first female pilot to shoot down an enemy plane, the first female pilot to earn the title of "ace," and the record-holder for greatest number of kills by a female fighter pilot. *(1921)*

Lydia Litvyak

Meriwether Lewis, co-leader of the Lewis and Clark Expedition that explored the Louisiana Purchase. (*1774*)

Meriwether Lewis

Music

Dennis Elliott, drummer for the rock band *Foreigner.* *(1950)*

Antonio Salieri, director of Italian opera in Vienna under the Hapsburg monarchy, remembered for his fictional portrayal as a rival of Wolfgang Amadeus Mozart in the stage and film production *Amadeus.* *(1750)*

Performing Arts

Andy Samberg, actor and filmmaker known for his digital shorts on *Saturday Night Live* and for the television series *Brooklyn Nine-Nine.* *(1978)*

Malcolm-Jamal Warner, best known for playing Theo Huxtable on *The Cosby Show.* *(1970)*

Christian Slater, actor whose best known films include *Heathers, Interview with the Vampire,* and *True Romance;* won a Golden Globe for his role in the television series *Mr. Robot.* *(1969)*

Edward Norton, actor nominated for Academy Awards for the films *Primal Fear, American History X,* and *Birdman.* *(1969)*

Madeline Stowe, actress known for roles in *Stakeout, Revenge, The Last of the Mohicans,* and *We Were Soldiers.* *(1958)*

Antonio Salieri, by Joseph Willibrord Mähler

Shelley Winters

Denis Leary, actor and producer known for the television series *Rescue Me* and for his role in the 2012 film *The Amazing Spider-Man*. *(1957)*

Patrick Swayze, actor and dancer best known for such films as *Dirty Dancing, Ghost,* and *Point Break.* *(1952)*

Elayne Boosler, stand-up comedienne and actress; first woman to get a one-hour comedy special on Showtime. *(1952)*

Martin Mull, actor known for such series as *Mary Hartman, Mary Hartman* and *Fernwood 2 Night*. *(1943)*

Robert Redford, actor and director whose best known films include *The Sting, All the President's Men,* and *Out of Africa;* won an Academy Award as Best Director for *Ordinary People. (1936)*

Gail Fisher, played Peggy Fair on the television series Mannix; first African-American woman to win a Golden Globe award. *(1935)*

Roman Polanski, film director and producer whose best known films include *Rosemary's Baby, Chinatown,* and *The Pianist. (1933)*

Shelley Winters, movie star who won two Academy Awards; best known films include *The Diary of Anne Frank, A Place in the Sun, The Poseidon Adventure,* and *The Night of the Hunter. (1920)*

Politics

Caspar Weinberger, secretary of defense under Ronald Reagan, indicted and pardoned during the Iran-Contra Affair. *(1917)*

Science and Mathematics

Luc Montagnier, shared the 2008 Nobel Prize in Physiology or Medicine for his discovery of the human immunodeficiency virus (HIV). *(1932)*

Liviu Librescu (ליביו ליברסקו), scientist and engineer, known for his heroism during the 2007 Virginia Tech shootings, in which he allowed his students to escape at the cost of his own life. *(1930)*

Klara Dan von Neumann, one of the world's first computer programmers and coders, primary programmer for the ENIAC computer, spouse of mathematician John von Neumann. *(1911)*

Sports

Roberto Clemente, first Latin American player to be inducted into the Baseball Hall of Fame, died in a plane crash while on his way to deliver aid to earthquake victims in Nicaragua. *(1934)*

Just Fontaine, French footballer (soccer player) who holds the record for most goals scored in a single edition of the FIFA World Cup. *(1933)*

Marge Schott, president and CEO of the Cincinnati Reds franchise from 1984 to 1999, known for her controversial remarks and ethnic slurs. *(1928)*

Burleigh Grimes, last major league pitcher officially permitted to throw a spitball; member of the Baseball Hall of Fame. *(1893) (Photo page 14.)*

Roberto Clemente 1962 baseball card

Caricature of Honoré de Balzac by Nadar (1850)

Who Died on August 18?

Business

Walter Chrysler, founded the automobile manufacturer Chrysler Corporation. *(1940)*

Joseph E. Seagram, founder of the Canadian whisky distillery of the same name. *(1919)*

Journalism and Literature

Robert Novak, conservative political commentator and journalist nicknamed "the Prince of Darkness" by his colleagues. *(2009)*

Anita Loos, novelist and screenwriter best known for *Gentlemen Prefer Blondes*. *(1981)*

Honoré de Balzac, French novelist and playwright credited as a founder of realism in European literature; his best known work is the multi-volume *La Comédie humaine (The Human Comedy)*. *(1850)*

Military and Government

Kim Dae-jung (김대중), president of South Korea, awarded the Nobel Peace Prize in 2000. *(2009)*

Subhas Chandra Bose, Indian nationalist leader known for his attempts to free India from British rule with the aid of Nazi Germany and Imperial Japan. *(1945)*

Genghis Khan, founder and Great Khan of the Mongol Empire, the largest contiguous empire in history. *(1227)*

Music

Scott McKenzie, singer-songwriter known for the 1967 hit single "San Francisco (Be Sure to Wear Flowers in Your Hair." *(2012)*

Elmer Bernstein, film score composer whose best known works include *The Magnificent Seven, The Great Escape, Ghostbusters,* and *Thoroughly Modern Millie. (1945)*

Performing Arts

Bud Yorkin, television producer known for his partnership with Norman Lear that created such sitcoms as *All in the Family, Maude, Good Times,* and *Sanford and Son. (2015)*

Don Pardo, radio and television announcer for such shows as *Saturday Night Live, The Price is Right,* and *Jeopardy!*; member of the Television Hall of fame. *(2014)*

Portrait of Genghis Khan by an anonymous court painter. The text is Genghis Khan's name rendered in Uyghur, which Genghis Khan established as the Mongolian Empire's official writing system.

Psychology

B. F. Skinner, behaviorist psychologist and social philosopher who considered free will an illusion; creator of the operant conditioning chamber, popularly known as the Skinner Box. *(1990)*

Religion

Alberto Hurtado, Chilean Jesuit priest and social worker, canonized in 2005 as Chile's second saint. *(1952)*

Science and Technology

Eli Whitney Blake, member of the National Inventors Hall of Fame for his mortise lock and his stone-crushing machine; nephew of cotton gin inventor Eli Whitney. *(1886)*

Sports

Josephine D'Angelo, left-fielder for the All-American Girls Professional Baseball League, set a record for fewest strikeouts in a single season. *(2013)*

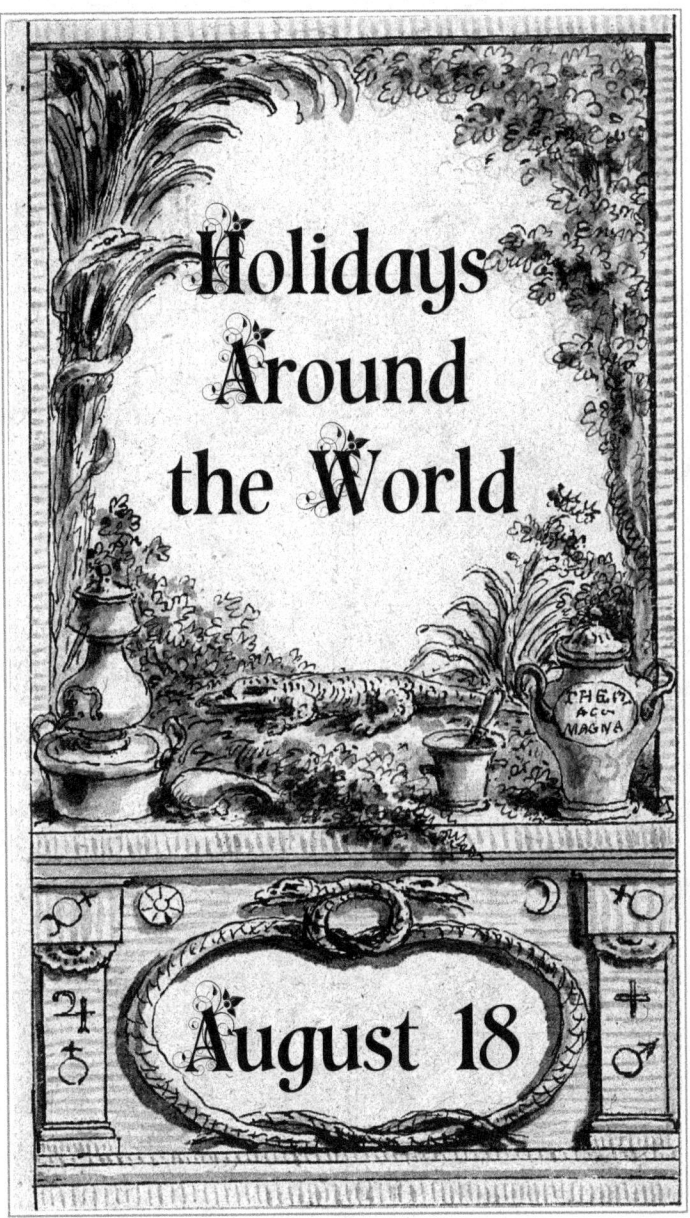

Holidays
Around
the World

THEM
ACN
MAGNA

August 18

King Mongkut (Rama IV) of Thailand, by John Thomson — for Thailand's **National Science Day**

Holidays Around the World

If you're looking for a reason to take your special day off, you should know that every single day is a holiday somewhere in the world! Here's some of what you can celebrate on August 18!

General Events

Wan Witthayasat Haeng Chat (Thailand)
National Science Day in Thailand commemorates the prediction and observance of an 1868 total solar eclipse by King Mongkut, a champion of science and technology in that country. He is best known in the west as the king in *The King and I*.

Arbor Day (Pakistan)
Many nations encourage the planting of trees on a special day. In Pakistan, the National Tree Plantation Day (قومی شجر کاری دن) is celebrated on August 18.

Day of the Macedonian Army (Macedonia)
Many nations honor their military on a special day. Macedonia's date was chosen to commemorate the country's first organized battalion in World War II, the Mirče Acev, formed August 18, 1943.

Long Tan Day (Australia)
Commemorating Australian valor during Battle of Long Dan, Vietnam, August 18, 1966.

Food Holidays

In the United States, almost every day of the year is dedicated to a particular food. (Some other countries do this also, but not every day.) Sponsored by manufacturers, retailers, farmers, or simply fans, these days are often proclaimed by the President, Congress, state governors, or mayors. Given that there are more different foods than days of the year, some days honor more than one kind of food!

August 18 is **National Ice Cream Pie Day** according to Foodimentary, **National Pinot Noir Day** according to Wikipedia, and **National Fajita Day** according to Brownielocks. That's a full meal, right there!

In addition, the entire month of August is used to celebrate numerous foods. Here's a list of what to eat in the month of August!

- National Catfish Month
- National Goat Cheese Month
- National Panini Month
- National Peach Month
- National Sandwich Month

Related to food, August is also Family Meals Month. If you're willing to share your ice cream pie, that is.

Pinot Noir grapes, for **National Pinot Noir Day** (Photo: Olivier Colas, CC BY-SA 4.0)

Honorary Months

Presidents, Congresses, and nations around the world issue proclamations recognizing particular months to honor certain causes. These events generally fall in August, though honorary months do come and go. Holidays established by states and nonprofit organizations are listed if verified. If not otherwise specified, all months are US. There is some variation from year to year; some celebratory months get added and others get dropped. Two places to get up to date information are the current edition of *Chase's Calendar of Events* or the website Brownielocks (www.brownielocks.com). Here are some honorary designations for August.

- American Adventures Month
- American Artists Appreciation Month
- American Indian Heritage Month
- Audio Appreciation Month
- Bystander Awareness Month
- Children's Eye Health and Safety Month
- Child Support Awareness Month
- National Children's Vision and Learning Month
- Digestive Tract Paralysis (DTP) Month
- Get Ready for Kindergarten Month
- Month of Philippine Languages (Philippines)
- National Back to School Month
- National Black Business Month

August is **Get Ready for Kindergarten Month**! This 1943 photograph is from a nursery school operated for women working in the war effort. (Photo: Marjory Collins for the Farm Security Administration, Office of War Information)

- National Breastfeeding Month

- National Immunization Awareness Month
- National Lawn Games Month
- National Minority Donor Awareness Month
- National Water Quality Month
- Neurosurgery Outreach Month
- Psoriasis Awareness Month
- Spinal Muscular Atrophy Awareness Month
- What Will Be Your Legacy Month
- Win with Civility Month
- Tomboy Tools Month
- Win With Civility Month

Religious Feast Days and Holidays

Each day in the year is considered a feast day for one or more saints. They are somewhat different in western Christianity (Catholicism and many forms of Protestantism) and in eastern (Orthodox) Christianity.

In *Western Christianity*, August 18 is the feast day of Saints Agapitus of Palestrina, Alberto Hurtado, Fiacre, Helena of Constantinople, and William Porcher DuBose (Episcopal Church).

In *Eastern Orthodox Christianity*, it is also the commemoration of the Holy Host of Paupers, Saint Macarius, Firminus of Metz, Daig Maccairill, Milo, Inan, and Christodoulus the Ossetian. (These are observed on August 5 by "Old Calendarists [1].")

---

[1] For an explanation of the Old (Julian) Calendar and the New (Gregorian) Calendar, see "What Day of the Week is August 18?"

Moveable and Multi-Day Events

Some events take place over a specific week or time period.
Some events occur on different days each year (such as
"fourth Saturday of a month"). These events sometimes
take place on August 18.

Third Monday
- Independence Day (India)
- Day of Hearts (Haarlem and Amsterdam, Netherlands)
- Discovery Day (Yukon, Canada)
- National Mourning Day (Bangladesh)

Third Friday
- Hawaii Admission Day (United States)

Third Saturday
- National Honey Bee Day (United States)

Third Sunday
- Children's Day (Argentina and Peru)
- Grandparents Day (Hong Kong)

Just for Fun

Anybody can make up a holiday, and many people do!
While none of these are officially recognized and some may
come and go, here are a few more holidays for August 18.

- Bad Poetry Day
- Mail Order Catalog Day
- Men's Grooming Day
- Serendipity Day

Quote of the Day

"Make haste slowly."

Augustus, first emperor of Rome
and namesake of the month of August

About
the
Month
of

August

"August," from the *Brevarium Grimani* by Simon Bening (c.1510)

August: The Eighth Month

In the parching August wind,
Cornfields bow the head,
Sheltered in round valley depths,
On low hills outspread.
— *"A Year's Windfalls," Christina G. Rossetti*

In ancient Rome, the month we know as August was originally known as *Sextilis*, meaning sixth. That's because the Roman calendar of the time had March as the first month of the year. It originally had only 29 days, but in his great calendar reform in 45 BCE, Julius Caesar added two days to the month. In 8 BCE, the month was renamed August in honor of Augustus, first emperor of Rome.

It's often claimed that Augustus stole one of February's days to add to his month, but the month already had 31 days long before Augustus became emperor. Augustus chose the month because it was the time of year in which he had accomplished some of his greatest triumphs, including the conquest of Egypt.

In both the Julian and Gregorian calendars, August is the eighth month of the year. It's one of seven months that have 31 days. During leap years, August and February start on the same day of the week; in non-leap years years, no month begins on the same day of the week as August. However, August and November always end on the same day of the week, regardless of the type of year.

In the Northern Hemisphere, August is a summer month, and in many European countries, the holiday month for most workers. In the Southern Hemisphere, August is the equivalent to February, deep in winter. No matter which hemisphere, August is a good month to spot a meteor; the Perseid Meteor Shower always takes place during the month.

August is also the month in the US that has the highest birthrate.

August in Other Cultures

The month of August has different names in different languages. Some nations use calendars other than the Gregorian, and their months may overlap with June. In lunar-based calendars, such as Islam, months move through the seasons. Still, many languages often have a word for August itself.

Albanian: Gusht

Arabic (Egypt, Sudan, Yemen): يونأغسطس (Aġustus)

Arabic (Levant): حزيراآب ('āb)

Arabic (Libya): الصهانيبال (hānībāl)

Arabic (Algeria and Tunisia): جوأوت (Ūt)

Arabic (Morocco): غشت (ġušt)

Azerbaijani: Avqust

Basque: Abuztu

Chinese: 八月 (Cantonese: baatyuht; Mandarin: bāyuè; Taiwanese: peh-goeh)

Croatian: Kolovoz

Czech: Srpen

Finnish: Elokuu

French: Août

German (Swiss): Auguscht (in other German dialects, it's just "August.")

Greek: Αύγουστος (Aúgoustos)

Hebrew: יאוגוסט (âvgûst)

Hindi: अगस्त (agast)

Hungarian: Augusztus

Irish (Gaelic): Lúnasa mí Lúnasa

Italian: Agosto

Japanese (traditional calendar): 九月 (kugatsu), 長月 (nagatsuki)

Korean: 팔월 (palweol)

Lithuanian: Rugpjūtis

Maori: Hereturikōkā

Old English: Wēodmōnaþ

Polish: Sierpień

Russian: август (Avgust)

Sesotho: Phato

Spanish and Portuguese: Agosto

Swahili: Agosti

Thai: Singhakhom

Vietnamese: 腸參 (tháng tám)

Welsh: Awst

Yiddish: אויגוט (oygust)

Zulu: uAgasti

August Sayings and Superstitions

Here are some sayings and superstitions associated with the month of August.

General Supersitions

"Agosto, mês do desgosto," or "August, the month of sorrow and grief." (Brazil)

"If a cold August follows a hot July / It foretells a winter hard and dry." (Farming)

If thunderstorms occur in early August, they will continue for the rest of the month.

Don't sail on the second Monday in August, because it was the day the ancient kingdoms of Sodom and Gomorrah were destroyed. (Old seafaring superstition)

If you bathe at midnight on August 1 (Lammas Day) in Lockmaur, Sutherlandshire, you'll be cured of all bodily ailments, but you're expected to repay the Spirit of the Lake with coin. (Scotland)

Wedding Supersitions

"August, better have waited." (Western Kentucky)

"An August bride will be agreeable, And practical as well."

"Married in August's heat and drowse/Lover and friend in your chosen spouse."

"Whoever wed in August be, many a change is sure to see."

The following days in August are considered auspicious for weddings: August 2, 11, 18, 20 and 30.

As for which day of the week to get married, that's easy.

> Monday for health, Tuesday for wealth,
> Wednesday best of all, Thursday for losses,
> Friday for crosses, Saturday for no luck at all.

A Regency wedding proposal

August Symbols

Birthstone: Peridot or sardonyx.

Peridot

Sardonyx (The ancient Cup of the Ptolemies, probably made in
Alexandria, Egypt, in the 1st Century CE)

Birth Flowers: Poppy or Gladiolus, both symbolizing strength of character, love, marriage, and family.

Vase with Cornflowers and Poppies, by Vincent van Gogh

Vase with Red Gladioli, by Vincent van Gogh

"August," by Eugène Grasset

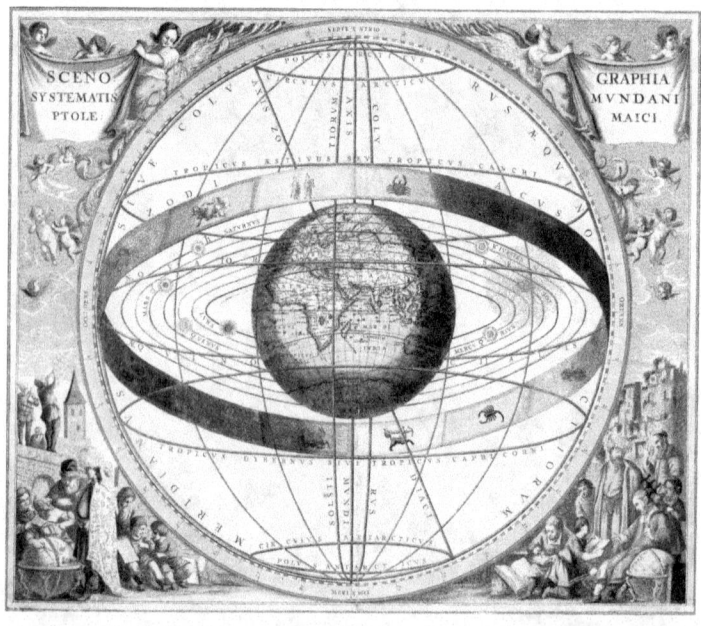

Scenography of the Ptolemaic Cosmography, by Johannes van
Loon, based on Andreas Cellarius's *Harmonia Macrocosmica,* 1660

August 18 Zodiac Signs

From the perspective of someone on Earth, the Sun appears to move through the sky throughout the year, along a path astronomers call the *ecliptic plane*. The ecliptic plane is divided into twelve constellations, known as the zodiac, based on traditionally observed patterns of stars. On your birthday, you can't see your constellation, because it's in the daytime sky.

The zodiac was first developed by Babylonian astronomers about 2,500 years ago. Because they were unaware that the Earth wobbles like a spinning top (known as *precession*), they didn't make allowance for the fact that the Sun's path through the zodiac changes over time.

That means there are now two sets of dates for your birth sign. The *tropical dates* are the original Babylonian dates; the *sidereal dates* tell you where the Sun actually appears as it moves along its annual path.

August 18, however, is one of the few dates each year in which both the tropical sign and the sidereal sign are the same: **Leo**.

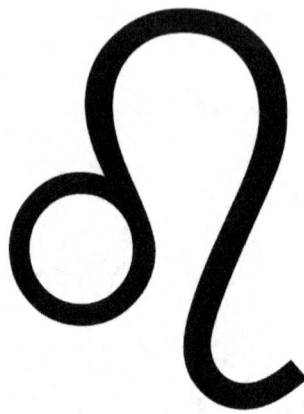

Leo

Tropical July 23 to August 22
Sidereal August 16 to September 15

Leo is one of the earliest recognizable constellations, with its stars forming a sickle or backward question mark. The Mesopotamians, the Persians, the Jews, and the Indians all had a name for the constellation that meant "lion." In Greek mythology, the Nemean lion was impervious to any weapons, but the hero Hercules nevertheless defeated it.

In astrology, Leo is a fire sign, suggesting that Leos are strong-willed and passionate. Leos are supposed to be compatible with Aquarius, Aries, and Sagittarius, but not with Gemini, Capricorn, or Pisces.

The Sign of Leo, by Giovanni Maria Falconetto
(Courtesy Palazzo d'Arco, Mantua, Italy)

Illustration by Edward Penfield

What Day of the Week is August 18?

On what day of the week does August 18 fall?

Surprisingly, this isn't an easy question. Because the calendar year is 365 days long (366 in leap years), it doesn't divide evenly by the seven days of the week.

Also, the Earth goes around the Sun in about 365-1/4 days, so a calendar tends to drift over time. That's why the same date falls on different weekdays in different years.

This is made even more complicated by a change in calendars that took place in 1582. Our modern calendar has its roots in ancient Rome, in a calendar reform conducted by Julius Caesar. Caesar commissioned mathematicians to attack the problem, and they came up with the idea of leap years, and thus standardized the calendar for centuries to come. This was called the Julian calendar.

Over time, however, the small errors in Caesar's calculation compounded. That's why Pope Gregory XIII commissioned the Gregorian calendar, used in most of the world today. Some countries converted in 1582, when the calendar was first developed; some converted later; other still haven't changed.

Gregorian and Julian aren't the only types of calendars. The Hebrew year, the Islamic year, and many other calendars are used in different parts of the world and among different people.

You can convert Gregorian dates to other calendars, including the Hebrew calendar, the Islamic calendar, and even the Mayan calendar by visiting the Fourmilab Calendar Converter at http://www.fourmilab.ch/documents/calendar/.

Chinese calendar systems are quite complex and have changed several times; a full discussion is far beyond the scope of this book. If you're interested, you can find information here: http://www.hermetic.ch/cal_stud/chinese_cal.htm.

On Names and Dates

Historians use "CE" (Common Era) and "BCE" (Before the Common Era) instead of the more common "AD" (Anno Domini, or Year of Our Lord) and "BC" (Before Christ), reflecting the fact that the year-numbering system established by the Gregorian calendar is used throughout the world in many countries not culturally Christian.

The CE/BCE designation dates back to at least 1708, and has been adopted as a standard by the United Nations and the Universal Postal Union. Because this series of books covers events and people of all nations and cultures, we use the CE/BCE terms.

The abbreviation "O.S." ("Old Style") on some dates refers to the fact that the Russian Empire did not switch from the Julian to the Gregorian calendar at the same time as the rest of Europe, and therefore some figures and events have two dates.

Also, in the Julian calendar in England in the 16th century, the year began on March 25 rather than January 1. To avoid confusion with Gregorian dates, dates between January and March were often written using both years.

People and events whose original names are not in the Western alphabet have their native names (where possible) in the appropriate script shown in parenthesis. If you are using an e-reader to access an electronic version of this book, all characters don't always display on all devices.

A 50-year brass perpetual calendar.

Quote of the Day

"Time is an illusion, lunchtime doubly so."

Douglas Adams,
from *The Hitchhiker's Guide to the Galaxy*

Notes
and
Credits

Timespinner
Press

Cartoon by John T. McCutcheon

Copyright, Credit, and Contact

Follow Us

Our blog "This Day in History" (http://
timespinnerpress.com/this-day-in-history/) features short
articles on events and people associated with each day, and
updates several times each week. Also subscribe to the
"Quote of the Day" at http://timespinnerpress.com/quote-
of-the-day/. You can get daily links by following us on
Facebook at TimespinnerPress, or on Twitter as
@sidewisethinker.

Contact Us

Find an error or a format problem? Want information about
the series, about us, or about when the volume for your
special day might be available? Please email us at
editor@timespinnerpress.com. (We also take requests if your
special day isn't yet complete. Please give us at least six
weeks' notice if possible.)

Sources

We owe a great debt to Wikipedia, which is our first stop for
research. We attempt to make independent confirmation of
all important dates and facts through a variety of other
sources.

Other sources we frequently use include the Library of
Congress; "on this day" listings from *Encyclopedia Britannica*,
the *New York Times*, and the BBC; Omniglot for the names of
months in other languages; *Chase's Calendar of Events*;
Brownielocks.com, Foodimentary, and, of course, the always
essential Google.

All art and photographs are either in the public domain, used under a Creative Commons license, or with a "fair use" justification, and most frequently come from Wikimedia Commons and the Library of Congress Prints and Photographs Division.

Attribution is provided where possible, or as requested by the copyright owner, or when there is particular historical significance, listed below. For information about any particular illustration or photograph, please contact us.

Credits

1. The cover painting is cropped from the cover of the official program for the March 13, 1913, women's suffrage procession in Washington, DC, created by the National American Women's Suffrage Association. It is in the public domain because it was first published in the United States prior to January 1, 1923. The image is courtesy Library of Congress Prints and Photographs Division, digital ID cph. 3g02996.

2. The illustration of the month of August used on the back cover is from the French Gothic illuminated manuscript *Les Très Riches Heures du duc de Berry* by the Limbourg Brothers, Jean Colombe, and an intermediate painter whose name is lost to history. It is in the public domain because its copyright has expired.

3. The box graphic used on the first page is from a 1916 pamphlet entitled "Divorce versus Democracy" authored by G. K. Chesterton, originally published in London by the Society of St. Peter and St. Paul. It is in the public domain in the US because it was published prior to 1923, and is in the public domain in all countries (including the country of origin) in which the copyright time is the author's life plus 70 years or less.

4. The graphic design for the section pages in this book is from a design originally created for a pharmacy label. It is

courtesy of Wellcome Images (ICV No 11073, photo V0010813), and is used here under CC BY-SA 4.0.

5. The photograph of Elizabeth Cady Stanton and Susan B. Anthony was originally taken circa 1900 and is in the public domain because its copyright has expired. The image is courtesy Library of Congress Prints and Photographs Division, digital ID cph.3a02558.

6. The cartoon "I did not raise my girl to be a voter" originally appeared in the October 9, 1915, issue of *Puck* Magazine, and is in the public domain because its copyright has expired.

7. The 1912 photograph of the Women's Suffrage Parade, New York City, in the public domain because its copyright has expired. The image is courtesy Library of Congress Prints and Photographs Division, digital ID cph.3g05585.

8. The 1915 illustration "The Awakening" by Hy Mayer is in the public domain because its copyright has expired. The image is courtesy Library of Congress Prints and Photographs Division, digital ID cph.3b49106.

9. The 1912 photograph of a women's suffrage headquarters in Cleveland, Ohio, is in the public domain because its copyright has expired.

10. The 1913 postcard supporting women's suffrage is in the public domain because its copyright has expired. The image is courtesy Library of Congress Prints and Photographs Division, digital ID cph.3b41501.

11. The 1783 watercolor of the Great Meteor as seen from Windsor Castle by Paul Sandby is in the public domain because its copyright has expired.

12. The photograph of an aircraft observer during the Battle of Britain is from the collection of the US National Archives and Records Administration (ARC 541899). It is in the public domain as a work prepared by an officer or employee of the US government as part of that person's official duties.

13. The official presidential portrait of Sukarno is in the public domain because its copyright has expired, according to Articles 30 and 31 of the Indonesian Copyright Law of 2002.

14. The photograph of RAF Hawker Hurricanes in flight is courtesy of the Imperial War Museum (CH 1499). It is in the

public domain as a photograph created by the UK government and taken prior to June 1, 1957.

15. The photograph of Luftwaffe Heinkel He 111s in flight is courtesy of the Imperial War Museum (MH 6547). It is in the public domain as a photograph created by the UK government and taken prior to June 1, 1957.

16. The photograph of Burleigh Grimes was taken circa 1916 and is in the public domain because its copyright has expired.

17. The 1906 portrait of Marshall Field is in the public domain because its copyright is expired.

18. The photograph of Lydia Litvyak is in the public domain according to article 1281 of Book IV of the Civil Code of the Russian Federation No. 230-FZ of December 18, 2006 and article 6 of Law No. 231-FZ of the Russian Federation of December 18, 2006.

19. The portrait of Meriwether Lewis first appeared in *Popular Science Monthly* in 1908. It is in the public domain because its copyright has expireed.

20. The 1815 portrait of Antonio Salieri is by Joseph Willibrord Mähler. It is in the public domain because its copyright has expired.

21. The publicity photograph of Shelley Winters is in the public domain because it was first published in the United States between1923 and 1977 without a copyright notice. Traditionally, publicity photographs are not copyrighted because of the way in which they are intended to be used.

22. The 1962 Fleer baseball card of Roberto Clemente is in the public domain because it was published in the United States between 1923 and 1963 and although there may or may not have been a copyright notice, the copyright was not renewed.

23. The caricature of Honoré de Balzac by Nadar was created circa 1850, and is in the public domain because its copyright has expired.

24. The portrait of Genghis Khan is by an anonymous court painter, and is in the public domain because its copyright has expired.

25. The rendering of Genghis Khan's name in Uyghur script was taken from Wikipedia. It is in the public domain because a simple rendering of text it is not subject to copyright.

26. The photograph of King Mongkut of Siam was taken in either 1865 or 1866 by John Thomson, and is courtesy of the National Library of Scotland. It is in the public domain because its copyright has expired.

27. The 2013 photograph of pinot noir grapes was taken by Olivier Colas, and is used here under CC BY-SA 4.0.

28. The 1943 photograph of a Buffalo, New York, nursery school for children of working mothers was taken by Marjory Collins for the Office of War Information. It is in the public domain as a work created by an employee of the US federal government. The original photo is in the collection of the Library of Congress, digital ID fsa.8d18633.

29. The painting "August" is from the *Brevarium Grimani*, circa 1510, and is in the public domain because its copyright has expired.

30. The 1815 woodcut of a proposal is in the public domain because its copyright has expired.

31. The photograph of an emerald cut peridot was taken by Michelle Jo, who released it into the public domain in 2009.

32. The photograph of the Cup of the Ptolemies was taken by "Clio20" and is used here under CC BY-SA 3.0. The cup is in the collection of the Bibliothèque Nationale de France.

33. The 1886 paintings *Vase with Cornflowers and Poppies* by Vincent van Gogh are in the public domain because its copyright has expired.

34. The 1886 painting *Vase with Red Gladioli* by Vincent van Gogh is in the public domain because its copyright has expired.

35. The 1886 painting *Vase with Cornflowers and Poppies* by Vincent van Gogh is in the public domain because its copyright has expired.

36. The 1896 illustration "August" by Eugène Grasset is in the public domain because its copyright has expired.

37. The celestial sphere is from *Scenography of the Ptolemaic Cosmography*, by Johannes van Loon, based on Andreas Cellarius's *Harmonia Macrocosmica*, 1660. It is in the public domain because its copyright has expired.

38. The fresco "Sign of Leo" by Giovanni Maria Falconetto was created between 1515 and 1520, and is in the public domain because its copyright has expired. It can be found in the Palazzo d'Arco, Mantua, Italy.

39. The 1906 automobile calendar is by Edward Penfield, and is in the collection of the Library of Congress Prints and Photographs Division. It is in the public domain because its copyright has expired.

40. The 50-year perpetual calendar photograph is in the public domain.

41. The cartoon by John T. McCutcheon is from his 1905 collection *The Mysterious Stranger and Other Cartoons* by John T. McCutcheon. It is in the public domain because its copyright has expired.

42. The painting *August* by Joachim von Sandrart is in the public domain because its copyright has expired. The original can be found in the Staatsgalerie im Neuen Schloss, Schleißheim, Germany.

License Description and Terms

Aside from material purely in the public domain, photographs and other material in this book are used under specific licenses permitting free use, usually with an attribution requirement. For full text and terms of these licenses, click or enter the appropriate links below. If you believe there is an error in the copyright status or attribution of any of these images, please email us.

- Creative Commons Attribution 2.0 Generic (CC-BY 2.0): http://creativecommons.org/licenses/by/2.0/deed.en

Timespinner
Press

August, by Joachim von Sandrart

Other Books from Timespinner Press

The Story of a Special Day
Michael Dobson

A series of (eventually) 366 volumes covering everything that happened on your special day! Events, births, deaths, quotes, holidays, and much more. It's like a birthday card they'll never throw away!

US$7.95 print / US$2.99 ebook.

From Plassey to Pakistan
Humayun Mirza

The history of British Colonial India and the formation of Pakistan from the unique perspective of the son of Pakistan's first president and last of the royal line of Bengal, Bihar, and Orissa! This unique historical document tells the inside story of this distinguished family, including the detailed story of the coup that toppled his father from power!

US$27.95 print

A Whole New Navy: America's War in the Pacific

Miles Durr

The most comprehensive and detailed description of America's naval war in the Pacific ever—every battle, every ship, every task force and every task group from Pearl Harbor through the Japanese surrender! A must-have for the collection of every World War II buff!

US$29.95 print

Improbable History: The Weird, the Obscure, and the Strangely Important

edited by Michael Dobson

From the birth of Western civilization to the rescue of Apollo 13, from the Leaning Tower of Pisa to Florence's Duomo, history has often turned on small, improbable details. Whatever happened to the ancient Samaritan people? Why did a fortuitous rainstorm allow the British to conquer India? How did an air raid in Italy lead to the development of chemotherapy? What happened when Albert Einstein met Adolf Hitler on the streets of Berlin? How did the Japanese manage to attack the US mainland using balloons? A cast of award-winning writers tackle some of the strangest tales in history!

US$19.95 print